Whale Shark

The World's Biggest Fish

by Meish Goldish

Consultant: Jenny Montague
Assistant Curator of Marine Mammals
New England Aquarium
Boston, MA

BEARPORT
PUBLISHING

New York, New York

Credits

Cover, ©Seapics.com; 2–3, ©Scott Tuason/Image Quest Marine; 4, Kathrin Ayer; 4–5, ©Norbert Wu/Minden Pictures; 6, ©James D. Watt/Image Quest Marine; 7BKG, ©James D. Watt/Image Quest Marine; 8 (inset), ©Kevin Aitken/Peter Arnold; 8–9, ©James D. Watt/Image Quest Marine; 10, ©Peter Parks/Image Quest Marine; 11, ©Flip Nicklin/Minden Pictures; 12, ©Jurgen Freund/Nature Picture Library; 13, ©Kevin Aitken/Peter Arnold; 14–15, ©James D. Watt/Image Quest Marine; 16 (inset), ©Kevin Aitken/Peter Arnold; 16–17, ©Flip Nicklin/Minden Pictures; 18–19, ©Andre Seale/Seapics.com; 20–21, ©Doug Perrine/Seapics.com; 22L, ©Pascal Kobeh/BIOS/Peter Arnold; 22C, ©Kare Telnes/Image Quest Marine; 22R, ©Mike Parry/Minden Pictures; 23TR, ©Kevin Aitken/Peter Arnold; 23BL, ©Norbert Wu/Minden Pictures; 23BR, ©Peter Parks/Image Quest Marine; 23BKG, ©Alstills/Bilderberg/Peter Arnold.

Publisher: Kenn Goin
Editorial Director: Adam Siegel
Editorial Development: Nancy Hall, Inc.
Creative Director: Spencer Brinker
Photo Researcher: Carousel Research, Inc.: Mary Teresa Giancoli
Design: Otto Carbajal

Library of Congress Cataloging-in-Publication Data

Goldish, Meish.
  Whale shark : the world's biggest fish / by Meish Goldish.
    p. cm. — (SuperSized!)
  Includes bibliographical references and index.
  ISBN-13: 978-1-59716-397-2 (library binding)
  ISBN-10: 1-59716-397-X (library binding)
  1. Whale shark—Juvenile literature. I. Title.

QL638.95.R4G65 2007
597.3—dc22

                              2006030597

For more information, write to Bearport Publishing Company, Inc., 101 Fifth Avenue, Suite 6R, New York, New York 10003. Printed in the United States of America.

10 9 8 7 6 5 4 3 2 1

Contents

Giants of the Sea

The whale shark is the biggest fish in the world.

A whale shark is about as long as a school bus.

Whale sharks can grow to more than 40 feet (12 m) long. They can weigh up to 30 tons (27 metric tons). Females are larger than males.

Warm-water Homes

Whale sharks swim in warm oceans near the **equator**.

These big sharks can dive deep down in the ocean.

Yet they also swim near the top of the water.

Whale sharks can be bigger than many kinds of whales.

Whale Sharks in the Wild

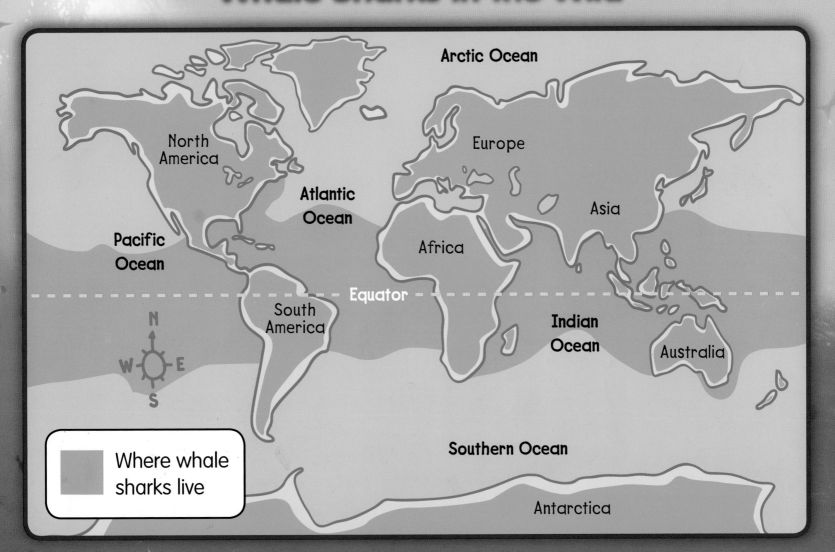

Arctic Ocean

Europe

Asia

North
America

Atlantic
Ocean

Africa

Pacific
Ocean

Equator

N

South
America

Indian
Ocean

Australia

W E

S

Southern Ocean

Where whale
sharks live

Antarctica

Big Mouth

A whale shark's mouth is huge.

It can be up to 5 feet (1.5 m) wide.

A hungry whale shark swims
with its mouth open.

Food and water pour
into the huge opening.

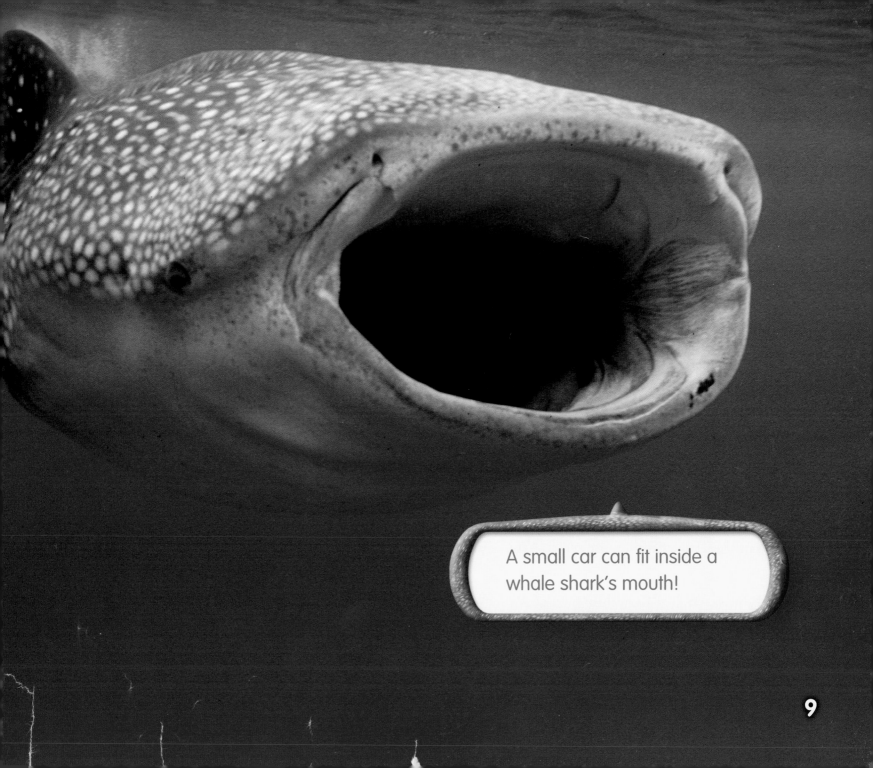

A small car can fit inside a whale shark's mouth!

Mealtime

The world's biggest fish eats the tiniest food in the sea.

The whale shark mostly eats **plankton**.

These tiny animals and plants float in the ocean.

Millions of plankton can fit in the whale shark's big mouth.

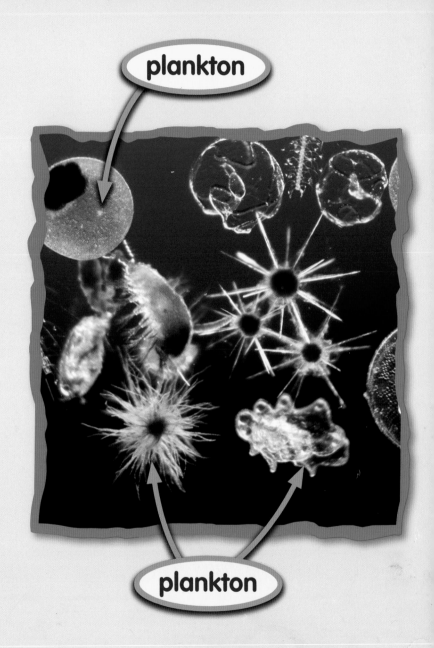

plankton

plankton

Whale sharks also eat sardines and other small fish.

Water In, Water Out

A whale shark swallows huge gulps of food and water.

The water leaves the shark's body through **gill slits**.

The food stays inside the shark.

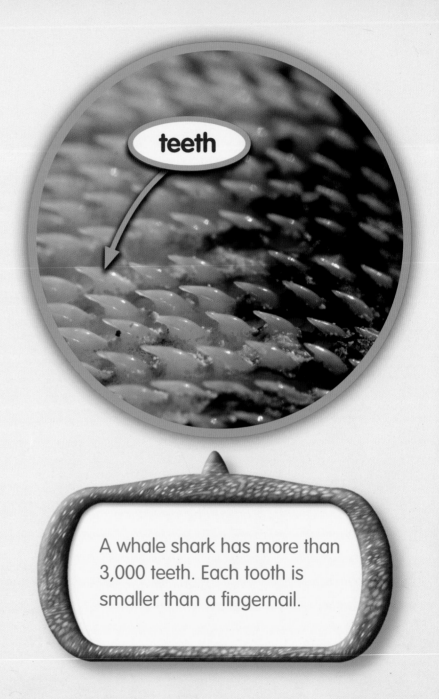

teeth

A whale shark has more than 3,000 teeth. Each tooth is smaller than a fingernail.

Life in the Sea

Whale sharks swim slowly.

They usually swim alone.

Whale sharks swim about 4 miles (6.4 km) per hour.

A Special Swimmer

A whale shark uses its **fins** to move in the ocean.

This giant shark can lie still in the water, too.

Most other sharks sink if they stop swimming.

The whale shark, however, can float.

fin

The whale shark and the basking shark are the only two sharks that can float.

Baby Sharks

Baby whale sharks grow in eggs inside their mother's body.

The animals hatch inside of her, too.

The live newborns come out of the mother and swim away.

Baby whale sharks are about 22 inches (56 cm) long when they are born.

A whale shark egg is the world's largest egg. It is 40 times larger than a chicken egg.

An Old Friend

No one knows for sure how long whale sharks live.

Many scientists think they live 100 to 150 years.

The whale shark is not just the world's biggest fish.

It is also one of Earth's oldest friends!

Scientists believe that whale sharks have lived on Earth for 200 million years.

More Big Fish

The whale shark is a shark, not a whale. Whales are mammals. Sharks are fish. Fish use gills to breathe. They also have a backbone. Most fish are cold-blooded and have fins and scales.

Here are three more big fish.

Basking Shark

The basking shark is the second largest fish in the world. It can grow up to 33 feet (10 m) long.

Oarfish

The oarfish can grow up to 30 feet (9 m) long.

Great White Shark

The great white shark can grow up to 21 feet (6.4 m) long.

Whale Shark: 40 feet/12 m

Basking Shark: 33 feet/10 m

Oarfish: 30 feet/9 m

Great White Shark: 21 feet/6.4 m

Glossary

equator
(i-KWAY-tur) an imaginary line halfway between the North and South Poles that runs around the middle of Earth

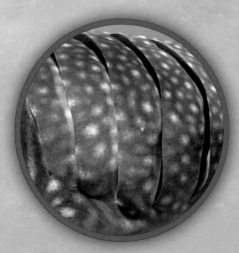

gill slits
(GIL SLITS) long, narrow openings on a fish's sides that let the animal get oxygen and through which water passes

fins (FINZ) flap-like parts of a fish that the animal uses to move and guide itself through water

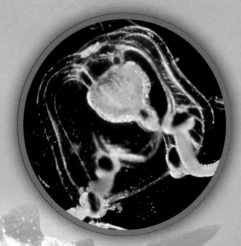

plankton
(PLANGK-tuhn) tiny animals and plants that float in oceans and lakes

Index

Read More

Crossingham, John, and Bobbie Kalman. *The Life Cycle of a Shark.* New York: Crabtree Publishing (2005).

Llewellyn, Claire. *The Best Book of Sharks.* Boston, MA: Kingfisher (2005).

Welsbacher, Anne. *Whale Sharks.* Minneapolis, MN: Capstone Press (1995).

Learn More Online

To learn more about whale sharks, visit **www.bearportpublishing.com/SuperSized**